For Micky, Fred,
Iona, Mandala and Jackie
T. B.

For Patrick, Joe, Alicia, Lewis
and, of course, Tiziana
J. B–B.

Consultant: Martin Jenkins

Text copyright © 1998 by Trudi Braun
Illustrations copyright © 1998 by John Bendall-Brunello

First U.S. edition 1999

Library of Congress Cataloging-in-Publication Data
Braun, Trudi.
My goose Betsy / by Trudi Braun : illustrated by John Bendall-Brunello. — 1st U.S. ed.
p.   cm.
Includes index.
Summary: Betsy the goose makes a cozy nest, lays her eggs, and tends to them until
her little goslings are hatched. Includes a section with facts about geese.
ISBN 0-7636-0449-6
1. Geese—Juvenile fiction.   [1. Geese—Fiction.]
I. Bendall-Brunello, John, ill.   II. Title.
PZ10.3.B745My   1999
[E]—dc 21   98-3456

4 6 8 10 9 7 5 3

Printed in Hong Kong / China

This book was typeset in Veronan and Soupbone.
The pictures were done in watercolor and colored pencils.

Candlewick Press
2067 Massachusetts Avenue
Cambridge, Massachusetts 02140

My Goose Betsy

Trudi Braun

illustrated by John Bendall-Brunello

CANDLEWICK PRESS
CAMBRIDGE, MASSACHUSETTS

My goose Betsy has
smooth soft feathers
to keep her warm and dry,

wide webby feet to swim with,

and a long strong beak for tearing
at grass or pecking up corn.

This is how she walks—
in a stately waddle,
her long neck stretched out
and her head held high,
staring sideways out of
beady blue eyes.

Squawk

Squawk

Honk

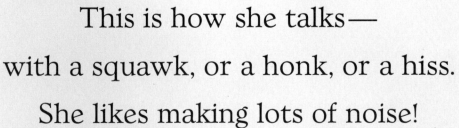

This is how she talks—
with a squawk, or a honk, or a hiss.
She likes making lots of noise!

My goose Betsy is building
a nest for her eggs.

Carefully, carefully,
she collects straw
with her beak

and makes a big pile
in the corner of the
goose house.

She sits on the pile
and shuffles her bottom
around to make
a snug hollow.

She lines it with fluffy down,
which she pecks from her breast.

When the nest is cozy and soft,
she lays her first egg.

Every two days,
Betsy lays another egg,
until her nest is full.

Then she settles down on top
to keep the eggs warm until they hatch.

Day
after day,
she sits very
still in the quiet
dark goose house.

Outside William the gander
is standing guard.
If anyone comes near,
he hurries toward them,
his wings spread,
his neck outstretched . . .

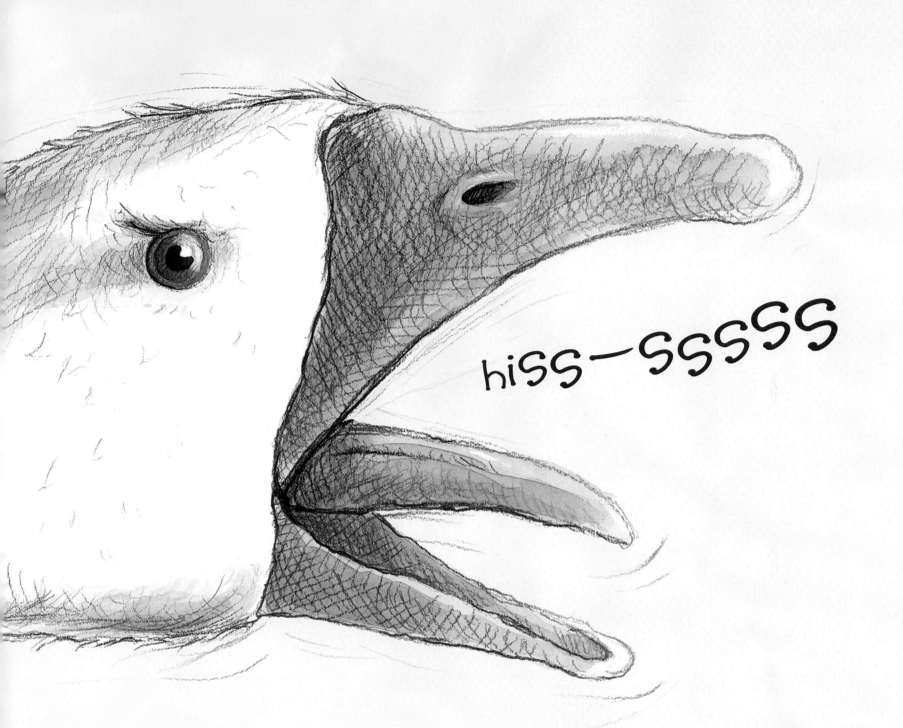

hiss—sssss

and his beak open wide
in a fierce hiss—sssss.

Once a day only,
Betsy gets off her nest.
Out she runs,
    calling to the gander.

She stands on one leg,
stretching the other
out behind her
like a ballerina . . .

and spreads her wings—
a lovely slow stretch.

Then she pecks at some grass
and has a quick splash
in the water tub.

But soon she hurries back to
her eggs before they get cold.

All the time Betsy is sitting
on her nest, her goslings
are growing inside
the eggs . . .

until one day,
the first gosling
is ready to hatch.

It begins to tap with its beak against
the hard eggshell,
and the shell
starts to
break.

The gosling taps some more.
The shell cracks open.

Now the gosling
starts to push
with its legs.

Tap, tap, tap.

Push, push, push.

What a struggle!

Suddenly, it is free.
The eggshell falls away,
and the gosling
tumbles
out into
the world,
out into the soft warm nest,
where Betsy is waiting
to gather it up under her wing.

One by one, all the eggs break
open, until her nest is full
of fluffy yellow babies.

My goose Betsy is a mother goose.

A few more Goose facts

The farmyard geese in this story are Embdens. They're descended from a kind of wild goose called the Greylag.

Laying eggs

Geese lay their eggs in the spring. They're white and about three times as big as hens' eggs.

Sitting on the nest

A goose will usually start to sit on her nest when she's laid eight to twelve eggs. It takes thirty days for them to hatch.

Inside the eggs

A gosling starts off as a tiny dot inside an egg. It feeds on the yolk as it grows, and by hatching time its body almost fills the egg.

Newborn goslings

A newly hatched gosling doesn't need to eat or drink—it just stays in the nest and is kept warm by its mother. After a few days, she takes all her goslings outside to find grass and water.

Growing up

Goslings are covered in fluffy yellow down at first, and start to grow white feathers when they're about a month old. After one year, they're ready to lay eggs and have babies of their own. Geese live for about thirty years.

Index

Look up the pages to find out
about all these geese things.